T0288408

Helping Hands

CONTENTS

NATIONAL GEOGRAPHIC
School Publishing
Hampton-Brown

Compound Words

Look at each picture. Read the words.

teapot

trashcan

backpack

sailboat

raindrop

driveway

High Frequency Words

- answer
- dear
- letter
- name
- say
- says
- write
- yes

Key Words

Look at the picture. Read the sentences.

Nov. 15

Dear Miss Lee,
Yes, I'll help with the cleanup!

Your friend,
Rose Ling

Two Letters

1. Rose got a **letter** from Miss Lee.
2. It **says** the city will have a cleanup day.
3. The letter asks if Rose will help.
4. She will **answer** the letter and **say** "**yes**."
5. Rose begins the letter, "**Dear** Miss Lee."
6. Rose says, "I'll **write** my **name** at the end."

What did Rose say she will do?

Phonics Games
NGReach.com

Cleanup Day

by Didi Mbwana

Look at this beach. It is littered with trash. People like to go to the seaside, but not if it is overflowing with trash.

So these people got a team of friends to clean the beach. They picked up the litter. They put it into big trashbags. Now people say the beach is a nice place to go.

Look around where you live. Has an overgrown lot become a wasteland? Have a cleanup day!

You need a plan. Here are the steps.

1. Pick a date and a place to clean.

2. Ask friends and grownups you know to help.

3. Work in the daytime. Finish before sunset.

When your plan is set, make a checklist. The list is important. It can help you and your teammates do the job.

Ask a grownup to check and see if the place where you live has rules about having cleanups. Follow the rules if the place says "yes."

Write letters to shopkeepers. Say that you've planned a cleanup. Ask if they want to help. If they answer "yes," you may want to ask them to donate trash bags or snacks.

Get the things you need such as trash bags and rakes. Don't forget gloves!

Put people on teams. Give each team a job. Teammates must work together. Tell them to stay close by each other.

May 20

Dear Miss Jones,

Thank you for donating 250 trash bags for cleanup day. We filled them all!

Thank you,

Sam Estes

After the cleanup, send thank-you letters to shopkeepers and teammates who helped. Write your name at the end of each letter.

The place is clean and neat now. The teammates are tired, but they can take pride in their hard work. What would you tell them about the great job they did? ❖

Compound Words

Read these words.

cleanup	trash	teammates	grownups	seaside
litter	follow	trashcans	wheelbarrow	

Find the compound words. Use letters to build them.

d a y t i m e

Talk Together

Choose words from the box above to tell your partner what the people clean up.

Teammates clean up the seaside.

Abbreviations

Look at each picture. Read the words and the abbreviations.

Doctor Dr.

Street St.

September Sept.

Friday Fri.

Mister Mr.

Madame Mrs.

High Frequency **Words**

answer
dear
letter
name
say
says
write
yes

Key Words

Look at the pictures. Read the sentences.

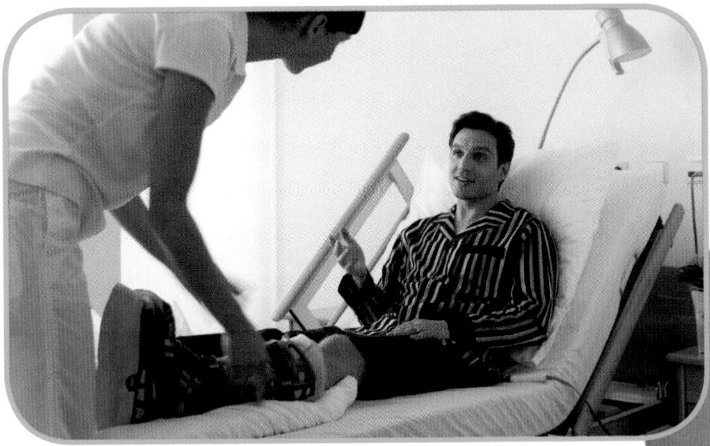

A Letter to Mr. Lee

1. Mr. Mike Lee got a **letter** with his **name** on it. This is what the letter said.
2. **Dear** Mr. Lee, Can you help me?
3. Dr. Kim **says** I broke my leg and need help.
4. I hope you can **write** an **answer** soon.
5. I hope you'll **say**, "**Yes**, I can help you!"

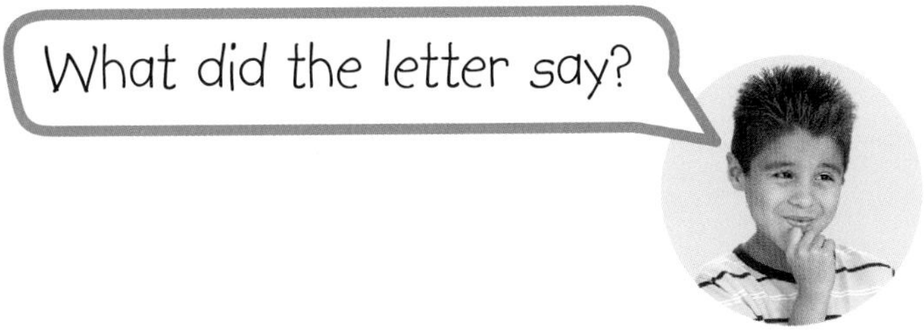

GO! **Phonics Games**

NGReach.com

All Kinds of Doctors

by Ana Martinez

Did you know there all kinds of doctors? They do different jobs. Here are just some of the jobs doctors do.

Dr. Lee will see you now.

When you get sick, you need to see a doctor. The doctor will look for an answer. He can help you get better.

Dr. Mack is in.

This is a different kind of doctor. He treats pets. He will see a cat or a rabbit. Yes, he will see a snake, too. This pet's name is Ms. Black.

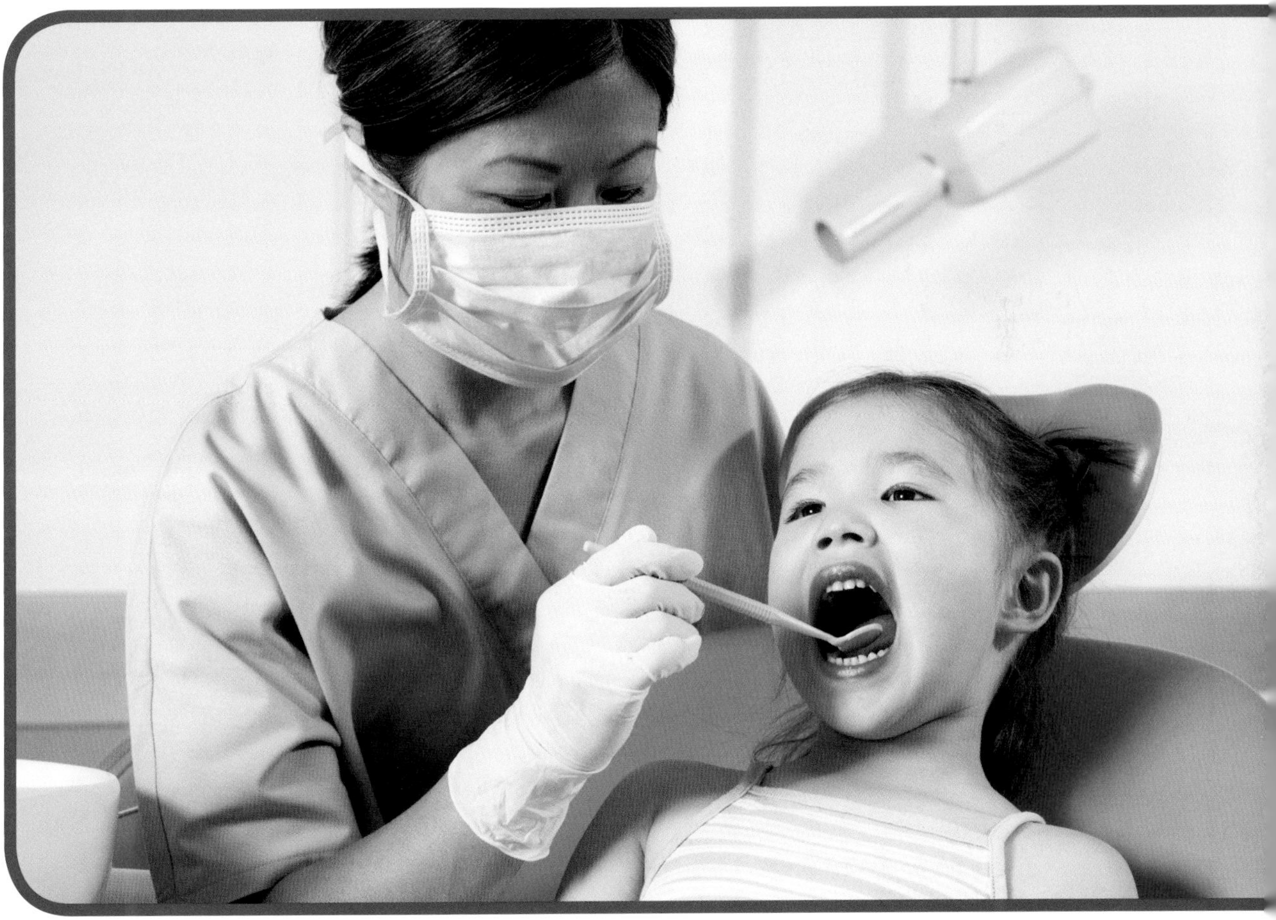

Dr. Ming says, "Open wide."

This doctor works with your teeth. She'll clean them and fix holes. Then she will show you how to brush and floss them.

Dr. Fitch will help you see.

If you need glasses, this doctor can help you. She will fit you with glasses. Then you can read the little letters on the chart.

Dr. Pratt says, "Come in!"

This doctor just takes care of little kids. She works on Main St. Mr. Hatch takes his baby to Dr. Pratt.

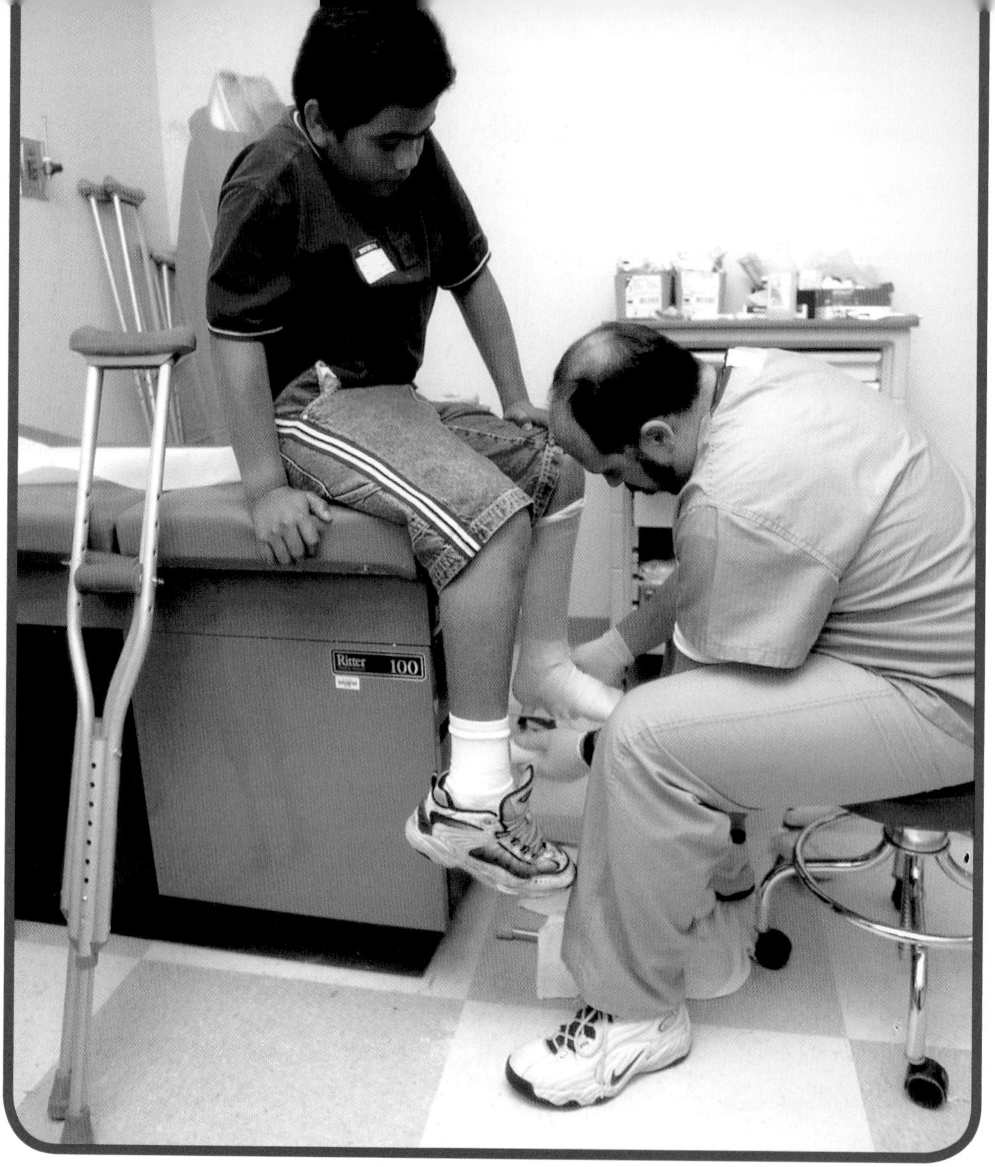

Dr. Rob will fix it.

This doctor is trained to fix broken bones. When that happens, a cast may be the answer. The cast helps the bone to mend.

Dr. Feller is in the lab.

This doctor works in a lab. She works with test tubes. She figures out how to cure sick people.

Dr. Golden looks inside.

The doctor has a way to see inside you. An x-ray helps him see deep inside. He reads the x-ray and says what he saw.

Dr. Nays can say, "Go!"

Some kids would like this doctor's job. She treats athletes. If a player gets bumped, she is there to help. She goes to all the games.

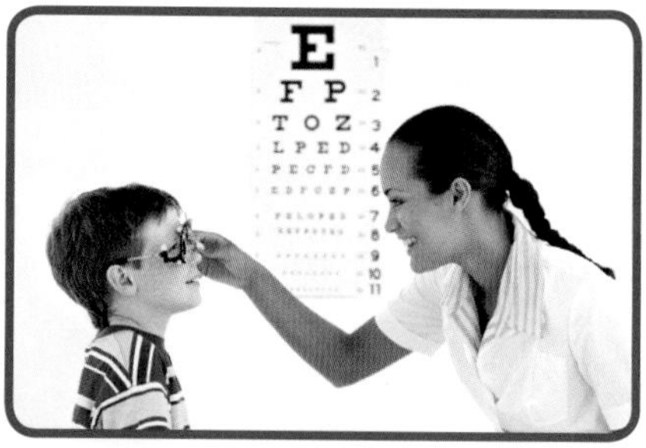

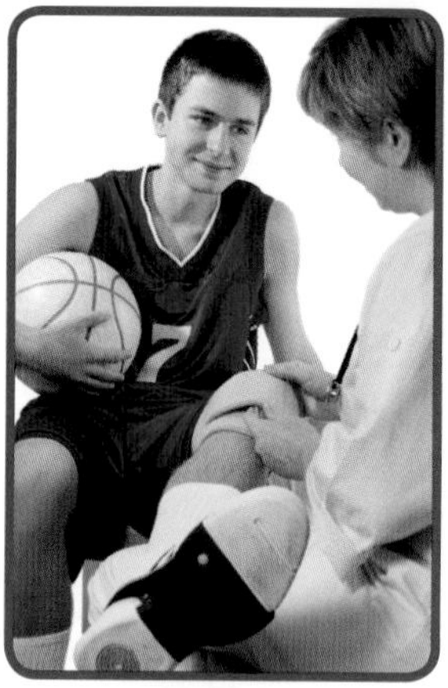

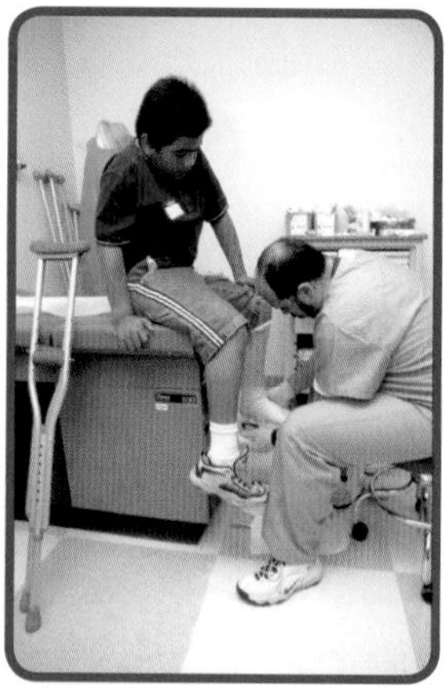

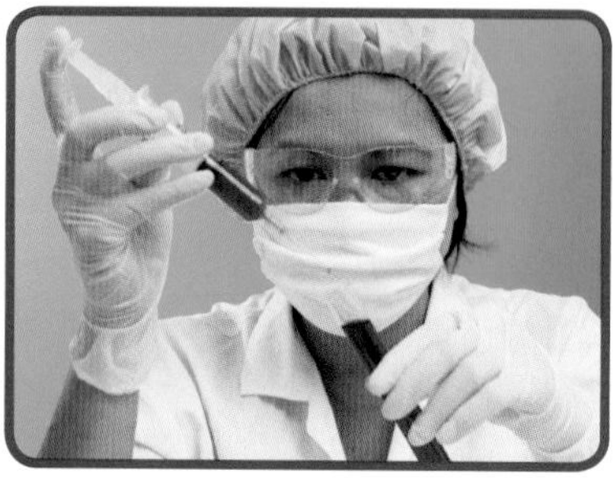

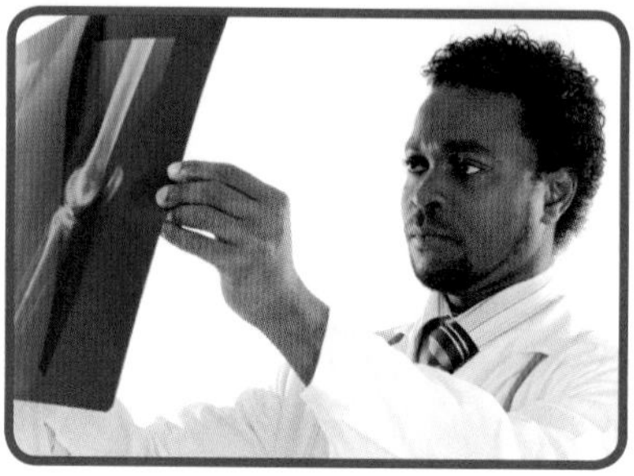

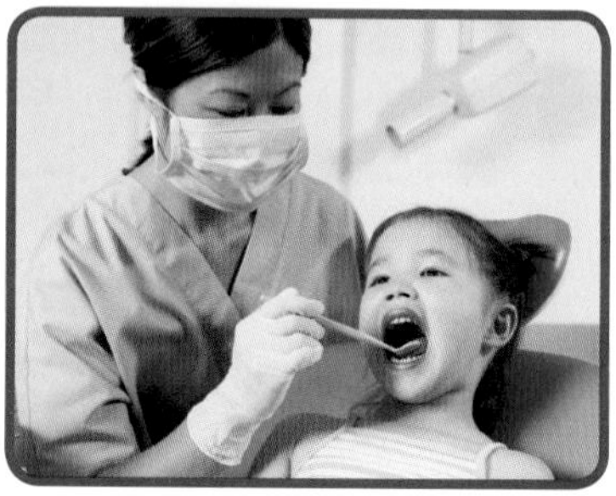

Maybe you'd like to be a doctor. Some day you may fix a bone or help a sick pet. You may be the doctor who figures out how to cure a cold!

Abbreviations

Read these words.

St.	Dr.	Mr.	do	me
Mrs.	W.	street	west	TX

Find the abbreviations. Use letters and periods to build them.

S t .

Talk Together

Choose words from the box above to tell your partner who helps.

Dr. Tran helps Mrs. Lopez.

Find Mrs. Pat Smith

Look at the pictures with a partner. Take turns reading clues. Then find Mrs. Pat Smith.

1. Her nametag says Mrs. Smith, not Mr. Smith.
2. She is not holding a letter that begins "Dear Mrs. Smith."
3. There is something in her backpack.
4. She has a notebook and a pencil.
5. She is not leaning on the trashcan that is overflowing.
6. She must answer her phone and so she can not write.

Mrs. Smith

Dr. Smith

Mrs. Smith

Mrs. Smith

Acknowledgments
Grateful acknowledgment is given to the authors, artists, photographers, museums, publishers, and agents for permission to reprint copyrighted material. Every effort has been made to secure the appropriate permission. If any omissions have been made or if corrections are required, please contact the Publisher.

Photographic Credits
CVR Ronnie Kaufman/Larry Hirshowitz/Blend Images/Corbis. **2** (bl) John Foxx Images/ Imagestate. (br) image100/Alamy Images. (cl) Thomas Perkins/iStockphoto. (cr) Elena Elisseeva/Shutterstock. (tl) Ingram Publishing/Superstock. (tr) MetaTools. **3** (b) Liz Garza Williams/Hampton-Brown/National Geographic School Publishing. (tl) Bohemian Nomad Picturemakers/Corbis. (tr) Noah Strycker/Shutterstock. **4** (inset) thumb/Shutterstock. **4-5** (bg) Floriano Rescigno/iStockphoto. **5** (b) ZTS/Shutterstock. (c) Creatas/Jupiterimages. (t) marylooo/Shutterstock. **6** Ralf-Finn Hestoft/Corbis. **7** Corbis. **8** (l) Luis Francisco Cordero/ Shutterstock. (r) Sean Locke/iStockphoto. **9** (bg) Monkey Business Images/Shutterstock. (inset) Luis Francisco Cordero/Shutterstock. **10** (bg) Radius Images/Alamy Images. (inset) Luis Francisco Cordero/Shutterstock. **11** (bl) Ingram Publishing/Superstock. (br) Luis Francisco Cordero/Shutterstock. (tl) Ken Cameron/iStockphoto. (tr) PhotoDisc/Getty Images. **12** (inset) Luis Francisco Cordero/Shutterstock. **12-13** (bg) Tim Pannell/Corbis. **13** (bg) Noah Strycker/ Shutterstock. (inset) stocksnapp/Shutterstock. **14** Tim Pannell/Corbis. **15** (b) cultura/ Corbis. (t) Liz Garza Williams/Hampton-Brown/National Geographic School Publishing. **16** (bl) BigWest1/iStockphoto. (br) Mel Curtis/Getty Images. (cl) Vadim Volodin/Shutterstock. (tl) Michael Krinke/iStockphoto. (tr) Richard Paul Kane/Shutterstock. **17** (b) Liz Garza Williams/ Hampton-Brown/National Geographic School Publishing. (r) Image Club. (t) altrendo images/ Getty Images. **18** (cr) Flashon Studio/Shutterstock. (bl) WilleeCole/Shutterstock. (br) 2happy/ Shutterstock. (cl) Boris Ryaposov/Shutterstock. (tl) Makarov Vladyslav/Shutterstock. (tr) Keith Bell/Shutterstock. **19** image100/Alamy. **20** Ariel Skelley/Getty Images. **21** Peter Dazeley/ Photodisc/Getty Images. **22** George Doyle/Getty Images. **23** iofoto/Shutterstock. **24** Spencer Grant/PhotoEdit. **25** william casey/Shutterstock. **26** Gelpi/Shutterstock. **27** Alexander Raths/ Shutterstock. **28** (bc) Gelpi/Shutterstock. (bl) william casey/Shutterstock. (br) Peter Dazeley/ Photodisc/Getty Images. (ccl) Ariel Skelley/Getty Images. (ccr) Alexander Raths/Shutterstock. (cl) Flashon Studio/Shutterstock. (cr) Spencer Grant/PhotoEdit. (tc) image100/Alamy. (tl) George Doyle/Getty Images. (tl) iofoto/Shutterstock. **29** Liz Garza Williams/Hampton-Brown/ National Geographic School Publishing.

Illustrator Credits
29, 30-31 Jannie Ho

National Geographic School Publishing
Hampton-Brown
www.NGSP.com

Printed in the USA.
Quad Graphics, Leominster, MA

ISBN:978-0-7362-8071-6

18 19
10 9 8 7